AND I'M NOT JENNY

performance :: writing

Tara Rebele

SLOPE EDITIONS

New Hampshire   New York   Massachusetts

Published by Slope Editions
www.slopeeditions.org

Library of Congress Cataloging-in-Publication Data

Rebele, Tara, 1972-
    And I'm Not Jenny : performance writing / Tara Rebele.—1st ed.
        p. cm.
    ISBN 0-9718219-5-X (pbk. : alk. paper)
    1. Performance art—Texts. 2. Feminism—Drama. 3. Women—
Drama. I. Title.

PS3618.E33A84 2005
812'.6—dc22
                            2005019006

Cover images ©2002 by Tara Rebele

Printed in the United States of America

9 8 7 6 5 4 3 2 1
FIRST EDITION

AND I'M NOT JENNY

performance :: writing

CONTENTS

9   And I'm Not Jenny

33   BeRemainBecome

41   Vice Versa

57   In Penumbral Flats

75   BODY/TALK/RADIO

85   *Production Notes*

AND I'M NOT JENNY

Characters:

20 Not-Jennys: women who are not Jenny describing their experiences not being Jenny

Not-Jenny 1:

I guess it must've been the summer before my third grade year when I realized I would never really be Jenny. That June, my family went on vacation to a resort in the Poconos and I introduced myself to all of the other kids as Jenny. It was great for a while, living a double life, regular old me back at the cabin with my family, moonlighting in the rec hall as Jenny. But it didn't last. There were three other Jennys there that summer and they were on to me from day one. "So, like, is Jenny your middle name or something?" one of the Jennys asked. "Are you a Jennifer? Or just Jenny?" one of the other Jennys wanted to know. I'm just Jenny, J-E-N-N-Y I lied. But they knew something was amiss, something about me just wasn't Jenny enough. My charade quickly began to unravel. There were only three Jennys on the roster for morning craft class and I wasn't one of them, but there I was, allowed to participate. A Jenny called to me one afternoon while I was out in the paddle boats with my father, "Jenny, Hey, Jenny. Jenny!" and I didn't respond. Another Jenny stopped by asking for Jenny and my mother told her "You must have the wrong cabin, there's no Jenny staying here." Finally, at the pool one afternoon, I got caught. My mother was calling me out of the water and after I ignored her for several minutes, she jumped right into the shallow end, grabbed me by the arm and gave me the old "First middle and last name, you are in deep trouble young lady." The Jennys jumped all over me. "You're not Jenny?" "You're not?" "You're not." "You're not Jenny!"

Not-Jenny 2:

There was always something very not Jenny about me. For one thing all of the Jennys were popular. And they had good hair and wore makeup and they were slim and hairless. I wasn't, didn't, didn't, wasn't and wasn't. Well, once I was. When I was 11, I wanted so badly to be like the smooth Jennys. I saved my allowance for two weeks, and one day after school I hopped on my Huffy Pink Thunder, pedaled down to JJ Newberries and purchased a big pink bottle of Nair. When I got home, I locked myself in the bathroom, sat on the toilet lid and read the directions. Hmph. Test patch. Allergic reaction. 48 hours. Whatever, I thought, as I gleefully slathered stinky pink cream onto my legs and forearms. Goodbye gorilla girl, I thought, hello hairless Jenny. I watched the clock. Left it on for a few extra minutes, just to play it safe. Then, I rinsed. Ooh burning. Oh not nice. Mmmm redness. Mmmm, ouch. Mmmm, the package read "will remove unwanted hair" not "causes great pain." So, turns out I was the one in x thousand who has a bad reaction to the product. And I was pink. And not a been-out-in-the-sun-a-little-too-long kind of pink. No. More like a shit-my-skin-is-on-fire-I-think-I-have-chemical-burns kind of pink. My parents made me go to school the following day, where the smooth, hairless, hypo-allergenic Jennys crossed and uncrossed their skinny, not chemically burned legs as they snickered and giggled at my expense. But, the burn went away after about a week. And I was hairless ... for about a month. Then, the hair grew back. Thicker and darker and even less Jenny than before.

Not-Jenny 3:

I guess deep down I've always known I wasn't Jenny. I mean, there was my first name, very not Jenny. My especially early menstruation debut on the Fourth Grade class trip. My glasses. And boys. Jennys liked boys and boys liked Jennys. Boys never liked me. I tried everything: did their homework, let them cheat off my quizzes, brought them candy and pursued them relentlessly: passing notes, calling on the phone, roller skating baaack and forth in front of their houses. Nothing worked. So, one Sunday afternoon when I was in eighth grade I took out my colored pens and splattered my schoolbook covers with I love Erics. On Monday, I waved my schoolbooks around where the Jennys would be sure to see them. They did. "Who's Eric?" they wanted to know. "My boyfriend." "Eric who?" they asked. "Oh, you wouldn't know him. He doesn't live around here. And besides, he's in high school." "Really, where'd you meet him?" they wanted to know. I lied and lied and lied, and Eric and I had just a fabulous romance for a few months. Then, before anyone realized they'd never actually seen Eric, I dumped him. He was just getting too clingy, too serious. He was madly in love with me, and I just didn't feel the same about him, so it was best to end it when I did, before he really got hurt. Eventually, an actual, living boy asked me on a date. I went. He liked me. So I fucked him. And when we were through with each other, I went on more dates, and I fucked them, too. And I went out with a lot more boys than the Jennys. And I fucked and fucked and fucked. And then, I fucked some more. And when I was about 29, I got tired of all the fucking. All that fucking fucking. So fucking tired. So I stopped trying to fuck my way to Jennyness and here I am, a walleyed, worn out, washed up former slut who's just not Jenny.

Not-Jenny 4:

No I've never been mistaken for Jenny. No sir. Not me. Nope. Never. I just ain't got one of those carrot-stick-eating-calorie-counting-power-walking-tae-bo'ing-size-four-stretchy-material-pants-by-Limited-wearing asses. No sir. Not me. I'm just not one of those booth-tanning-cell-phone-chatting-red-car-driving-black-bag-toting-shopping-by-appointment-always-smelling-like-hair-care-products gals. Nope. Never. I'm just too up-all-night-reading-oversleeping-mismatching-late-running-three-inch-pinching-quirky-thinking-coffee-drinking-thrift-store-buying-isn't-trying-has-weird-hair-and-hasn't-shaved-in-a-week-and-don't-care. No I've never been mistaken for Jenny. Guess this butt just ain't high enough. Hips don't swing wide enough. Pants ain't capris enough. Not 34-C enough. Heels ain't chunky enough. Style just ain't spunky enough. Body just ain't bam bam enough. Just not hot damn enough. No I've never been mistaken for Jenny. No sir. Not me. Nope. Never.

Not-Jenny 5:

When I asked, Jenny told me she was thinking about autumn outerwear. Wool scarves, hats, leather jackets ... I was thinking about throwing myself in front of a bus. Less chance to bounce off, and survive. No hoods, I said. Yeah, hoods are so last year, she agreed.

Not-Jenny 6:

Oh I'd just never make it as Jenny. I hate reduced-calorie, fat-free raspberry vinaigrette, Lean Cuisine frozen entrees and all things dietetic. I like burritos. With extra guac and sour cream. The fatter the better is my motto. I want it overstuffed and messy. I want it to erupt as I eat it. I want to lick cascading burrito juice from my frenzied feeding fingers. And when it's gone, when the last of the melted cheese has been scraped from the foil wrapper and the last stray shred of beef picked up and polished off, well then I want dessert. And I don't want caramel coated rice cakes, lowfat frozen yogurt or a fresh fruit dish. No. I want my nasty wrapped in plastic. I want Li'l Debbie Snack Cakes. I want Oatmeal Creme Pies. I want Star Crunch. I want Fudge Rounds. I want Zebra Cakes. I want Nutty Bars. I want gut ache. I'm not Jenny because I eat. I eat a lot. I eat for hunger. I eat for pleasure. I eat for pain. I eat to fill my empty. And I can't. So I'll just keep on eating.

Not-Jenny 7:

Jenny? Jenny's easy. Jenny works at a rewarding job. Jenny is career driven. Jenny is a go-getter. Jenny dresses just so. Jenny married "Mr. Right." Jenny carefully planned the birth of her 2.5 children to coincide with the company's annual "downtimes." Jenny can, therefore, plan combined birthday parties, order 2.5 cakes, invite 12.5 children, hire one clown, purchase one piñata and rent one bouncer. Jenny's 2.5 are tidy BabyGap poster children who can sit still for at least as long as Sunday service. Jenny's youngest child, .5, wears the same color nail polish as Jenny on her toes, which Jenny applies while .5 sits on the Baby-Bjorn potty hoping for poop. Jenny's oldest, Mr. Right Jr., is an honor student at Green Valley Elementary, which proud parent Jenny boasts on the shiny bumper of her luxury SUV. Jenny's middle child is not spectacular and Jenny simultaneously dislikes and coddles her because of this. Mr. Right does not like middle child, whose average marks and unruly hair disrupt the "perfect family" portrait, but he pretends to for Jenny's sake. Children, after all, are important to Jenny. They make her well rounded. They look good, hair combed, all dressed in white, silver-framed upon her desk, facing out.

Not-Jenny 8:

Well, I'm not Jenny. And I've never even been close to being Jenny. And it's not like I ever even pretended I could be Jenny if I tried. No. I've always known. I knew before I ever saw myself in a mirror and saw the blazing purple splotch across my right cheek. Before my parents explained the term "birthmark." Before Mandy in First Presbyterian Pre-K asked, "Ooh. What happened to your face?" and the teacher said, "Shh. Now Mandy, don't be rude." Before I created the elaborate tale of my alien abduction, the surgical implantation of a microchip in my skull that would allow the aliens to spy on humankind, the branding of my face by the extraterrestrials so when they returned to earth I could be easily spotted and reclaimed. How I was chosen because as an infant I showed signs of genius and special telepathic powers … How my secret powers and alien connections could really fuck up some little third grade twerp if he didn't stop calling me "Smooshed grape face" and "Weirdo." "Ooh. What happened to your face?" I knew before I never made it as a "teacher's pet" despite my straight A's and excellent behavior. Before the party invitations didn't come. Before the spinning bottle never landed on me. "Ooh. What happened to your face?" "Shh. Now Mandy. Don't be rude." Before the end of high school when I began to say, "It's a birthmark, asshole, and how do you explain that nose?" Before the scholarship applications that requested a photo, along with my flawless transcript. Before the other girls on my dorm floor rushed. "Ooh. What happened to your face?" Before my roommate got knocked up and left school. Before Lisa took her place. "Shh. Now Mandy, don't be rude." Before we stayed up all night talking. Before she told me she thought my birthmark was striking and made me "interesting." Before we started sleeping together. "Ooh. What happened to your face?" Before I dumped her for this guy I met in Anthro. Before he dumped me. Before many other dumpings and being dumpeds. Before graduation. Before numerous job interviews. Before someone told me I could probably have some sort of surgery or something, if I wanted … "Ooh. What happened?" "Shh. Don't be rude."

Not-Jenny 9:

I'm not Jenny. Jenny doesn't take it in the ass.

Not-Jenny 10:

Jennys don't have recurrent visions of self-mutilation. I do. Ergo,
I must not be Jenny. Because this happens to me a lot. The image
comes, flashes over and over: pink razor descends on ankle bone,
pulls upward, digging. Bleeding begins. Shower water enters
wound. Stinging. Blood streams, meets water, swirls down drain.
And over and over again: pink razor descends ...

And I can't turn it off. It repeats and repeats and repeats. And
it happens to me a lot. It happens when I am in bed with the
wrong man. And so, I say to this man, I think we shouldn't see
each other anymore. I say, Don't take this personally. It's just
that when we fuck I imagine I am being sliced by razors. I say,
No. It doesn't get me hot.

I say, Trust me, you'll be better off. I say, I have some serious
"issues."

I say, I'll never be Jenny. My shrink says these images serve as
a "physical representation of my pain." I think it might be nice
to be beaten once in a while.

Not-Jenny 11:

Not a Jenny. Nope, never a Jenny. Well, not unless you're a sweet little old lady—then a Jenny. Or family. Family gets away with Jenny. Or maybe a cute guy with some redeeming qualities who I'll nicely, but firmly correct. Ahem, it's Jen-nifer. But only once. Was a Jenny for a while. Well, I tried it, anyway. Tried J-E-N-N-I-E. Tried J-E-N-N-I. Tried J-E-N-N-Y. Just not a Jenny. Not an in-Jenny, anyway. Not a hanging out at the mall Jenny. Not a preppy shirt and khakied catalog style Jenny. Not a skinny Jenny. Not a blonde or even brunette Jenny. Not a bubbly Jenny. Not a two faced smile at you now and stab you in the back two minutes from now because I'm a fake little bitch Jenny. Like, not Valley Girl Jenny. Not a got a car for my sixteenth birthday Jenny. Not a going steady Jenny. Not a perfect pretty petite Jenny. Not an "in" Jenny. Nope. Tried J-E-N-N-I-E. Tried J-E-N-N-I. Tried J-E-N-N-Y. Changing the spelling didn't fix it. Didn't make me popular, or even liked. Didn't get me a boyfriend. Didn't change that I was thick as a stick with no fashion sense and nappy hair. Didn't erase my sneer. I was a Jenny with nothing to show for it. Ahem, it's Jen-nifer.

Not-Jenny 12:

It was 11:37 am, April 23, 1987, when my aspirations to Jenny-ness were just shot out of the sky like … some hunted waterfowl or something. Bang. I could have been another Jenny. Had the hair, the figure, a little Clearasil and I could pull it off. The wardrobe was always a crimp. My mother believed in thrift and sale rack shopping. Back to school for me meant trudging through musty church basement buck-a-bag sales, Salvation Army outings and squeezing into those sale rack clothes Mom was so pleased about the savings on at the end of the season the previous year, before that unanticipated growth spurt. This was pre-capris trend, when they were called highwaters and they got you noticed but not in that modish sort of way that one wants to be noticed. And thrift store chic had yet to hit. But I was clever and for the most part could work around the horrors that hung in my bedroom closet. My older sister, Lisa, had a job and bought her own clothes. Once in a while she'd take pity on me and throw a few hand-me-downs my way. Sometimes I'd leave for school a little early and stop at my friend Melissa's house to borrow an outfit. Usually I got by. I was never quite stylish enough, but I wasn't a freak show, either.

So, April 22nd. Melissa heard from Hilary, who'd heard from Jenny, that Jason D., the ultimate Jason in our school, who I'd recently worked with on the group Social Studies project, was thinking of asking me to the Spring semi-formal after class eighth period the next day, but … But what???? He wasn't quite sure, because he'd never seen me "dress up" at school like the other girls, and did I even own a skirt or a dress? Melissa told Hilary to call Jenny to tell her to call Jason to tell him that not only did I own several skirts and dresses that I didn't wear to school because they were so much more "mature" than what the other girls wore, but that I was actually planning to wear one the very next day. The pressure was on.

Fact is, I did own several "mature" outfits, as in they'd probably been owned by someone's grandmother who died and donated her estate to Goodwill before my mother got to them and thought they'd be just lovely on me for those more formal occasions, that my undersized jeans and slightly yellowed armpits secondhand blouses just wouldn't do — Lisa's high-school graduation, my cousin Margaret's wedding in August, maybe I'd even go to a school dance this year. Over my dead body I thought as I smiled thanks and ran upstairs to stuff it in the back of my closet, then weep.

Lisa. Lisa was swank. Lisa, whose job at the mall got her a hefty discount, had a room full of "mature," no, make that flat out sexy, dresses and shoes. Sexier than anything I'd ever seen on the Jennys. We struck a deal. On Friday night I'd flip the switch on mom and dad's "curfew alarm clock" — you know, set twenty minutes past curfew so they'd wake up if she didn't get home in time to shut it off — so she could stay out for a big party at The Pit. In exchange, she hooked me up with a knock-out dress and some pumps for school the next day. I was set. Fast forward to 11:36 am. Leaving the lunchline, tray full of government issued mac-and-cheese food product in hands, following Melissa to our usual table. Enter Jason D. I look at him. He looks at me. Walks past. "Wow, you look great today," he says. Swooning. Lack of experience in high heels. One step, two steps, wobble, wobble. Wipe out. 11:37 am. Everyone laughs. Everyone, including Jason D. Everyone but me. I do not laugh. I do not get asked to the semi-formal after class eighth period. Over my dead body. Quack.

Not-Jenny 13:

Jenny? Uh-uh. Not in this life. This ho-hum housewife life. Run-down runaround momma snoozing through routines. poopy diaper. feeding. cleaning. food prep. poopy diaper. feeding. laundry. peepee. feeding. what's that smell ... treading treading treading. dreading. poopy diaper, feeding. sleep sleep no sleep no sleep blissed out stressed out best thing's ever happened. who am I who are you who am I who are you we are we are we are we. sitter? yeah. oh no gimme my baby back ... grow up. no stop it. grow up. no don't. get off my breast. give my body back. no. no. nurse til you're thirty. just one long nap, I'll bounce back. floors swept. dishes done. casseroles cooked. baby's sleeping like a baby. momma's rubbing a few off thinking about the grocery list.

Not-Jenny 14:

There are no Jennys here. There are morning groups. And bubble gum pink walls. And meds. No belts, shoelaces, glass, sharp eating utensils ... Regular bowel movements are encouraged. And caffeine is a privilege for the closest to well. I would lose a few toes, maybe just the smallest few, for a strong, bitter cup. I think I saw the shell of a Jenny here once. But the Jenny was gone. Starved or purged, long before the skin skulked about this wing. Vacuous. Beyond hunger. The shell is gone now, too.

Not-Jenny 15:

It's not like I haven't tried to settle down with one guy. I have. Lots of one guys. But it never lasts. I just can't do long-term monogamy. And it's not like I have a wandering eye. No, more like a fickle clit. I get bored easily. I never leave them for someone else, I leave for the prospect of someone else, someone new, a novelty. Novelty gets me wet. Same old same old, does not. Doesn't matter how much I think I'm in love or how many adventurous new games we play. The same cock that delighted me so those first few times will bore me to tears two months later. And guys don't always take this so well either. They take it so fucking personally. I try to explain. I've tried everything I can think of to keep it going. I've tried fantasy: "Okay, now baby, when you come home tonight, pretend your name is Ricky and we've never met before … No baby, it's not that I don't love you. No, I don't want to replace you with some Ricky. Just your dick. Well I don't know how I'll pretend it's not you. Maybe I just won't look at it … Don't worry, baby. You just go have a good day at work. I love you. You come home Ricky …" Oh, how I have tried. But it ain't happening. I was really elitist about this for a while. Fancied myself "better than" the wives' club, more sexually aware, fulfilled. Figured they wouldn't know a big bad orgasm if it bit em in the ass, which sometimes helps. But then my friend Jenny, smiling perfect Jenny who's happily married to a great guy, of fucking course, told me, she's never been more satisfied. In fact, they've been fucking like bunnies for five years and she still gets off at least once every time. Lucky. Bitch.

Not-Jenny 16:

I'm not. I'm not. I'm not not not. Not. Not her. Not her twin. Not her older or younger sister. Or daughter. Or cousin. And you haven't met me somewhere before. And I'm sure you could've sworn when you approached me ... And I probably do look familiar, because apparently I do really look like somebody. Or everybody. But I don't know who the fuck that is and I'm sick of smiling politely, nodding no. You must have me confused with someone else. I'm quite certain we've never met ... I'm an only child. I'm not from around here. No, I'm not her. I'm not anyone but me, fucking generic me.

Not-Jenny 17:

I'm not a Jenny, but sometimes I imagine fucking one. Pretty femmy little Jenny. Long lustrous hair. Stairmaster ass. Salon-tanned, no lines. Waxed legs. Groomed pubes. Manicured. Actually, that's what always kills it for me. Those fucking nails. And it starts so sweet ... the seduction, the first awkward kiss, the ensuing tongue-teasing-showing-other-tongue-what-it-might-do-to-one's-lucky-clit kissing, bare breast fondling, nipple pinching, playful nibbling, tongue descending, belly button tickling, down, down, playful pause, down again, mouth to muff, tongue on clit. Hair in teeth, break for removal. She to me, hands on thighs, up, up. Aaaggh shit! Stop. Keep your daggers away from my coochie, honey. And that's that. Those fucking nails. Every time. Can she masturbate without great pain? Is she into pain? I'm not into pain. What about porn stars? How do they do it day in and day out? Is there a way to work nail trimming into foreplay? Can she even dial a phone or type with those things?

Not-Jenny 18:

I ain't a Jenny. But I knowa one. Works down to Debbi's Tan and Video three or four nights a week. Gets ta use the booths for free. She's wicked tan and bleached blonde and wears tight t-shirts and has a different nail color every shift and sometimes little gems or glitter, too. Every guy in town wants to fuck her, including my boyfriend. I seen the way he looks her up and down and up and down again every time we go in to rent a movie. And we only rent when Jenny's working. And I might's well not exist. He pretends he don't like her. Calls her things like "the stuck-up slut," "Little Miss Fake and Bake" and "the blonde video store bitch." But I know it's cos she won't give him the time a day. Won' give any of em the time a day. Moved here a coupla years ago with her Momma. Takes night classes when she aint working at Debbi's and is gonna be a Medical Office Assistant. Just don't want nothing to do with the local boys. She's gonna have herself a career. Get outta this shithole town. Oh how it pisses em off they can't get in her panties. Every time her name comes up they go back and forth 'tween imagining they've got a hold a her fine tan ass and pretty titties and cussin her out and getting downright mean and crude bout the poor girl. Ain't her fault she's so damn pretty and I sure wouldn't sleep with one of these losers if I didn't have to. Wonder if they know how stupid they sound calling her a slut like that when, fact is, she wouldn't even think of hitting skins with a single one of 'em. Dumb fucks.

Not-Jenny 19:

I have this rash. When I first started itching, there were these little red bumps all over my skin. So, I looked up skin rashes on the internet and thought my bumps fit the description of this rash, petechiae: bleeding into the skin. Not good. Upon realizing, quite suddenly and unexpectedly, that I was probably dying, I began to freak. I became nauseous, panicky. Then depressed. I looked up the various conditions — Septicemia, Lupus, Leukemia, Idiopathic Thrombocytopenic Purpura — matching my symptoms, that I was just now discovering were actual symptoms of something — irritability, lethargy, agitation, fatigue — I just thought it was because I don't sleep enough and spend my days strung out on espresso. But no, bona fide symptoms of many very serious illnesses ... I weighed the pros and cons of being diagnosed with each. Mentally prepared myself for all of the worst case scenarios. Waited two grueling weeks to get in for an appointment and the doctor gave my bumps a quick glance and said, "Looks like flea bites. Do you have a pet?" "But what about petechiae? Pinpoint red bumps? Bleeding into the skin? Look. It doesn't blanch with pressure." "It's scabbed," the Doc said. "Have you been scratching?" The doc assured me that my red bumps did not even closely resemble petechiae, which look like blood blisters, that they were really nothing more than insect bites. That, really, despite what I'd so certainly diagnosed myself with online, they were just flea bites. And since last month my colon cancer turned out to be the effects of too much caffeine and some pre-menstrual cramping, and a few weeks before that I escaped certain death from a brain tumor when my persistent headaches turned out to be the result of an outdated contact prescription, might I lay off the WebMD for a while, and perhaps consider some sort of herbal anxiety remedy, like Kava Kava ... Oh shit. Do you think I have anxiety? I wonder what that's a sign of.

Not-Jenny 20:

Well, yeah I went through a phase when I was young where I really wanted to be Jenny. I mean, who didn't? Of course I also wanted to be Joan Jett for a while. Yeah, when I listened to "I Love Rock N' Roll" for the first time, I was on fire. I knew that I was destined to become a rock star. And suddenly Jenny just wasn't so cool. Not when I was going to be a rock star. I didn't realize that I couldn't sing. No, when I sang I heard the next Joan Jett. And so I listened to that album hundreds of times over and I memorized every word and I sang til it hurt day after day after school. And I was loud. Volume was never my problem. My mulish voice and inability to carry a tune, those were problems. But not volume. Oh no. And I was convinced that I rocked out. And my family had to listen to me day after day after school, before school and on weekends. Finally, in the car one afternoon, after I'd sung "Crimson and Clover" over and over, my mom broke down. "You might not want to rule out college," she said, "because you're never going to make it as a singer." I got red hot and rockin mad. I ripped through the hardware store at her heels, firing Joan Jett tunes at the back of her head, as loud as I could. She bought me a blank cassette. Back at home, I locked myself in my bedroom, got out my boom box, popped in the tape, pressed record, let loose on its built-in mic, held my breath during rewind and hit play. And then I cried. A lot. And I put "I Love Rock N' Roll" on auto-reverse and sunk into my bean bag chair to writhe. And that cassette still spoke to me. It said, "Wear tight leather pants." It said, "Get a really bad spiky haircut." It said, "Dress all in black." It said, "You can be a badass, little girl." It said, "Jenny who?"

BeRemainBecome

Characters:

five unnamed women, identified by the make-up each applies

Performer:

a woman seated in front of a Remington True-to-Light Deluxe Lighted Make-up Mirror who wears no make-up at the beginning of the performance but applies each item with its corresponding monologue

All agree in recognizing the fact that females exist in the human species; today as always they make up about one half of humanity. And yet we are told that femininity is in danger; we are exhorted to be women, remain women, become women.

—Simone de Beauvoir

Foundation:

I've been Buff Beige since I was 14 ... going on seventeen years now. And I'm not about to change just 'cause that "specially trained" cosmetics representative at Sheila's party says it's the wrong shade for me. "Honey, you're a Summer," she told me. "Buff Beige is really best for Autumns, it just washes you out. You look like a corpse for christssake! Why don't you try something a little more you ... like a Pink Beige or maybe a Deep Rose Beige?" Because I am Buff Beige. I have always been Buff Beige. Once, and just once, I bought True Beige. The store was out of Buff. True looked pretty close. I figured I'd give it a go since it was either that or nothing at all — and that's a really frightening prospect ... So I tried the True. And it just wasn't me. Or maybe it was a little too me — a little too rosy, a little too girlish, a little too shy. Not a me I'd put out on the streets, that's for sure. I'm shooting for pale, severe, assured. Now, to get it right, it takes me about twice as much Buff as it used to. It's hard to get to that perfect finish, one that won't give me away when I need it most. Lately it's been real hard. I'm trying to get tougher in my relationship. But ya' think he's gonna buy my "shape up or ship outs" when I'm dawn-tinted like a timid schoolgirl? Hasn't yet. Oh I've threatened to leave many a time ... But anyway. Buff Beige is who I wanna be, and no poofy haired "beauty consultant" is gonna come riding up in her powder puff pink Caddy with her color charts and assorted brush sizes and tell me any different 'cause she thinks she knows what suits me best. I don't need to be anymore me than I already am.

Concealer:

Now this little stick really does the trick: flawed to flawless with a few quick dabs. Fantastic, isn't it? I mean, not that I'm *severely* blemished or anything ... I just have a few "problem areas" that need a little extra cover. I'm just trying to strike a balance between what is and what could be. Now my mother was the real whiz with this stuff. Step Daddy Two'd come home drunk and pop her a good one and she'd go right into town next morning to see about her errands, chatting it up with anyone and everyone—Step Daddy Three liked to call her "the Gab"—and not a one would notice. Mother taught me that no matter what you've got behind closed doors beating you up or bringing you down, well you've just gotta straighten your shoulders, put on your face to meet the faces, and get on. Took me a while to really get it. Used to be I'd wear my bother on my sleeve. Thought it might help me pin a good man. Sometimes my being broken *would* inspire a need to fix. And I'd spend a few good months sobbing on strong shoulders, weltering in my bygones. Then I'd get tired of being indulged, urged, encouraged and coddled because I wasn't really looking for salvation, anyway. Now I just never let them see me unstitched. They can just crack me like the shell that I am and come tomorrow morning I'll look as good as new. I been gluing pieces long as I can remember. Of course, the façade falls fast first time they see your scars.

Eye Make-Up:

Women wearing only underwear ride the outside of city buses. Tell you "inner beauty only goes so far." Perhaps a better bra is what you need.

Blush:

And a little color to the cheekbone brings the face to life, gives it that "sun-kissed" look, a youthful, healthy glow. Not that I need it. I'm getting my period so I'm already a little rosy. Funny huh, every morning I rouge my cheeks, because someone has said that this is something men will find attractive. But the one time of the month I look this way naturally, I'm lucky my boyfriend doesn't just up and flee the country. And it's really too bad 'cause I don't get bitchy ... I get horny. Increased blood flow or something. But it doesn't do me much good with Mr. Hemaphobia. So this'll be the fourth visit from "Aunt Flow" since we moved in together. First few were pretty ugly. He calls it my "curse" and says the bleeding thing makes him *squeamish* and will I please dispose of my "feminine products" somewhere other than our bathroom wastebasket and won't I try, just try, to be a little more understanding and not go flaunting my womanhood where he and anyone else he might invite into our home, into our bathroom, who might happen to peer into our trash, or actually reach in and unwrap one of my thinly disguised little toilet paper wads might discover the secret of my menstruation and where the dog may happen upon one such wad and drag it out into the living room to chew ... and so I returned from work that evening to find one used tampax, shaken, shredded and strewn about the futon and my *squeamish* boyfriend, sequestered in the back bedroom waiting for me to "dispose of my disposables" and clean up before he'd come out and he won't, to this day, sit on that futon and he had a near breakdown when I made it up as a bed for our houseguests. It's not like the tampon is still there, and I soaked and washed the cover. Perhaps we should just burn it. I think we could never have children. Me and my *squeamish* boyfriend. Imagine those six weeks or so of postpartum hell. And if we had a daughter ... Why do I even bother? Here I am flushed, warm and willing. And come seven o'clock I'll be sitting by myself on the futon, while my *squeamish* boyfriend cuddles up on the recliner with the dumb dog. If a bitch is not in estrus, she's just not receptive. She'll bite the male when he comes around, trying to mount. Women are receptive throughout their cycle, because our brains are so big. So what gives? It's not like I'm gonna sour the cream or spoil the meat. I mean, forgive me my fecundity …

Lipstick:

Some days my look just screams "swollen labia." Maybe I really wanna fuck or I really wanna get fucked. Maybe I just need a shot of validation. Or maybe I'm lonely or I'm bored or I've just got a yen for some good head. On those days, I won't step foot outta this house until I ooze "Screw me." And it works. I'll notice them noticing. "See me," I'll purr. I am ripe. I am woman. I am absolute sex. And they will. They will see me. They'll see exactly what I want them to see. They'll read in the red of my lips, "I seek consumption." And they will take. And I will give, give, give til he's standing at the door saying "I'll give you a call." And you can be damn sure a trace of my "Cherries in the Snow" is gonna follow him home. I always leave my mark. Maybe I'm an egoist. Or maybe I need an ego lift. Maybe I really didn't want to fuck at all. Or maybe I really did. Maybe I just can't take another fucking night alone with myself. Or maybe sex is just how I know ...

[Walks away from vanity.]

What do you want from *your* mirror?

Vice Versa

Characters:

Una: the character in the first person

Trece: the character in the third person/the image in the mirror

Cue Card Holder: the masked person who stands next to the mirror, raises large cue cards to face the audience

This piece is written for one person to perform the roles of both Una and Trece. The switch from Una to Trece is indicated when the performer confronts her image in a mirror, thus viewing the audience through her reflection, and switches voice from the first person to the third person.

ALL CAPS indicates content of cue cards.

There is a full-length mirror facing the audience. Cue Card Holder stands next to the mirror holding large cue cards. When Cue Card Holder raises a new card, there is a break in action long enough for the audience to read the card. During the break, the performer freezes in place, then resumes after the break as if never having stopped.

Una:

[Skipping onstage with her hands cupped in front of her as if carrying a bug.]

I'm bringing home a baby bumble bee,
won't my mama be so proud of me,
I'm bringing home a baby bumble bee —
Shit! That little fucker just stung me!

[She opens hands, drops bee, stomps on it. Faces audience.]

I feared the bee until I squashed it.
Feared that li'l bee until I squashed it dead.
I usually only bite if I'm asked nice. *Real nice.*
And I usually like my bees contained,
where I can keep a close eye on 'em.

When I was a kid, I used to cut holes
in the tops of peanut butter jars,
then run around my yard stomping on bumble bees,
not hard enough to kill 'em though,
just kinda quick to stun 'em for a minute.

I'd scoop 'em up and put 'em in the jars
that I'd fill with fresh grass and dandelions.
Then I'd wait for 'em to make me some honey.
I'd talk to 'em, give 'em names, fresh flowers,
and not one of 'em ever gave me any honey.
But it sure didn't stop me from trying.

When I got older I finally learned
the difference between bumble bees and honey bees.
You'd think my parents might've told me about that back then,
but no, they just let me run around,

stompin' bees with bare feet, trying to pet them,
thinking if I could make 'em like me,
they just might make me some honey
to put on my peanut butter sandwiches.

But no, my parents never said a word,
they just pulled out the stingers and gave me an antihistamine
every time one of my little pets stung
cuz bee stings make me swell up like a blimp.
No one ever thought to tell me "Una, you're allergic
to bees, they sting you, you cry, you hurt
and the damn things are never gonna give you any honey."

No one ever told me that 'bout friends, lovers or life, neither.
I always have to learn things the hard way.
I feared that bee until I squashed it.
I like my bees contained. And I sure like my honey.

BEE CONTAINED

I wanna taste my honey.
Mmm mmm mmm licking my sweet sweet honey.
I only feared that bee til I squashed it.
Someday I'm gonna grow wings of my own,
gonna fly fly fly so high above … beyond …

WHAT GOES UP MUST COME DOWN

Someday I'm gonna bite when I'm not asked.

REAL NICE

Someday, I'm gonna remember who I was yesterday
and know who I am today.
And they'll get together for honey tea
and maybe they'll be okay.

Holding hands they'll go skipping
down the sidewalk, looking
for tomorrow, next week, next month, next year ...

[Una turns toward mirror, sees her reflection.]

You again?

SHE PREFERS TO DANCE ALONE

I didn't invite you, Trece.

NO PARTNER TO LEAD, SHE JUST DANCES
CIRCLES AROUND HERSELF

I don't need you, ya know. I can be alone.
I can be like Castor without Pollux. Ginger
without Fred. Yeah, I can dance alone. I am ...

[Looks in mirror.]

Who am I?

[Looks away, puzzled.]

SHE USUALLY DANCES AROUND
TOUGH QUESTIONS, TOO

I am the queen bee.
I am a Gemini.
I am Una.
I am a lone dancer.
I am Una and
I am a lone ...

Trece:

The answer was not stated in the form of a question.

THIS IS JEOPARDY

Una:

Who is Una?

DOUBLE JEOPARDY

Last night I was Dorothy, clicking
together the heels of my ruby reds.
There's no place like home,
There's no place like home.
There's no place ...

HERS IS THE THIRD HOUSE ON THE LEFT

[Una faces the mirror, switches to Trece.]

Trece:

Last night the Wizard got pissed and dropped Una back to the yellow brick road on her ass. Seems she didn't know what she wanted. He started grumbling about women and their indecisiveness.

TRECE SAID SOMETHING ABOUT HIS GENDER STEREOTYPING

He said he was just a Wizard, not a miracle worker.

THEN SHE BROUGHT UP HIS NAPOLEON COMPLEX

Sure, he can grant a few wishes, spring for some glittery pumps, cab fare, but that's about his limit.

THE YELLOW BRICK ROAD ... A DOOMED FORAY

And Una, well, that Una's no innocent li'l Dorothy and the wizard's no psychotherapist. Besides, therapy never seems to work for Una.

QUEEN OF DENIAL

She's always looking for the quick fix.

AND SOMEONE ELSE TO INJECT HER WITH IT

Always falling in love with the idea. And, like her little bees, dying every fall.

PEOPLE WOULDN'T <u>FALL</u> IN LOVE
IF IT DIDN'T HURT TO LAND

[Points to card holder.]

Cynic!

[Facing reflection again.]

Like her precious queen, she kills them off one by one. Leaving them dead. Gutless.

Una:

No. Maybe that's how it *was*,
maybe I've fallen a few times,
but I'm getting back on my feet now.

STILL WEARING THOSE TACKY PUMPS, TOO

Moving forward. Leaving that old me behind.

MUST BE HARD WALKING AWAY
IN THOSE HIDEOUS THINGS

This time's gonna be different.
I'm better off now. This time
nothing's gonna stand in my way.
Old friends were bringing me down anyway.

Trece:

Never her fault. How can it be?

SHE DOESN'T KNOW WHO SHE IS

Born color blind, poor thing, only dreams black and white. Knows
there's a pot of gold at the end of the rainbow, just wouldn't know
how one rainy day could differ from any other. She's been walk-
ing around on her hands for so long. Blood rushing to her head,
heart slowly draining … afraid to let her feet touch the ground.
Afraid they might land her in quicksand. And so sick of herself
that she hides from her.

SHE'S GOTTA GRIP THE PRINCIPLE OF POLARITY

She's only a fraction of what she could be. A quarter of that half
that could combine to make her whole.

Una:

A quarter? Can you spare a quarter?
Cuz I've just gotta reach out and touch someone.
I need to let my fingers do the walking.
I've gotta call home, cuz there's no place like ...

HASN'T BEEN HOME SINCE LAST YEAR

I gotta call ahead cuz I'm bringing home my baby
bumble bee and they'll need to set an extra place
at the table for me and my honey ...

Trece:

She thinks definition can be found in another.

SHE READS THE DICTIONARY

Sometimes she knows better.

BUT SHE HASN'T QUITE COME TO TERMS

Like when lovers introduce her. "I'd like you to meet *my* partner,
Una. "

THIS PROPERTY BELONGS TO ...

Turns tail and runs away as fast as those little legs can carry her.
Such a mercurial sort …

GEMINIS ARE RULED BY MERCURY

Follows that scattered head of hers. Una tells 'em all to go to hell
and if that doesn't work she'll just drive them there herself.

MERCURY IN GREEK = HERMES

Hasn't felt a pulse in so long, probably doesn't even remember
she has a heart. So mutable. So capricious. So confused. Keeps
thinking she can go home and the little girl with the bee sting is
just gonna whisper truth in her ear and she'll walk away changed.
Thinks there's a secret can fix everything if only she knew …

Una:

Oh we're off to see the wizard …
Yeah, *we*. This time I'm traveling
with my three monkeys.
And when we see the wizard,
we're gonna ask him for some eyes,

SEE NO

some ears,

HEAR NO

and a voice,

SPEAK NO

and there won't be a secret anymore.
When I bring home my baby bumble bee
will my mama be so proud of me?

Trece:

She's allergic to bees. Puffs up like a zeppelin. Never learns.
Let her damn bees kill off her last love. Smothered: she couldn't
breathe enough for 'em both.

Una:

Miss Mary Mack Mack Mack
all dressed in black black black
too bad it's gone gone gone,
I'd like it back back back.

Trece

When she wants something so mechanical she oughta just look
away and stick to that battery operated lover that fits so nicely
in her purse ...

IT'S A MINI-PEARL

Una:

No, what I really want is to grow a stinger of my own.

Trece:

She wants the power to hurt. Best defense is a good offense.

SHE WANTS LOVE

[Trece turns to Cue Card Holder.]

Same thing.

[Cue Card Holder sticks out tongue at Trece.]

CYNIC

Una:

I'm so sorry, baby. Mama never told me
not to play with my bees. So very sorry, baby,
but could you please just give me that stinger
now before I forget what it is I wanted?

FEAR THE BEE

I know I shoulda squashed that bee when I had the chance.
I just wanted to taste your honey, baby,
but I couldn't get close enough without it stinging.
So now I'm growing my own wings, gonna fly fly fly ...

SOLO THIS TIME

Trece:

Yesterday catches up with today,

FORGIVE NOT FORGET

sets sights on tomorrow.

Una:

Stingers lead to antihistamines
which only bring the swelling down.
Closest I've come to god
or salvation was a green and yellow pill.
Fucking monkeys stole my fix,
spilled my secrets and left me outside looking in.

Trece:

She knows who I am.

Una:

Yes, but who am I?

Trece:

Una.

ANSWER IN THE FORM OF A QUESTION

Who is Una?

THIS IS FINAL JEOPARDY

Una:

I am Una. And I'm bringing home my baby bumble bee.

EMBRACING THE PRINCIPLE

And I'm clicking my heels
cuz there's no place like home
and I'm really gonna go find it.
There's no place like home.
There's no place like home.
There's no place like home.

OBJECTS IN MIRROR MAY BE CLOSER
THAN THEY APPEAR

[Una's cheek is pressed to glass of mirror.]

Mirror, Mirror on the wall,
who's the fairest *one* of all?

You are, Una.

[Leans into reflection then turns away from mirror.]

In Penumbral Flats

Characters:

Lucia: live performer

Mother: video projection

Mental Health Professional (MHP): cardboard cutout with audio feed

Note: Lucia begins in the light in order to look back at her shadows. The initial Summer section of the piece chronologically follows the final Spring section. This should be indicated in production.

The movement sequence between seasons is indicated in {} and should occur in a circular, perhaps spiral, pattern. The movement sequence at the end of the initial Summer section should break from the pattern. Percussion rhythms may accompany the movement sequences, paced according to the speed of the movement; if percussion is not used, some noise would be appropriate.

SUMMER

Lucia:

It isn't unpleasant as one
might expect
sitting up late
on the sofa
with the ghosts
preferable even
to years spent
refusing
to be
haunted.
One could blame
the wind
were there any
to be had.

Mother:

Lucia. Turn off the lights. It's late.

Lucia:

Late but not

MHP:

Medication compliance.

Lucia:

every second
again
every
the heaviest of

Mother:

Lucia. The lights. We'll have a fire. I've read about those lamps.

MHP:

Breakthrough episodes.

Lucia:

Every second.

So when you stand
in the light
your shadow
lurks.
Lest you forget
yesterday
you were

Yet when darkness

there's no shadow
of the shadow
no trace

to long
and long
it lasts
if one
lasts
long
enough

point A erased
again

This is the better

MHP:

Maintenance is crucial. Regular patterns. Monitor moods.
Continue treatment. As directed.

Mother:

You haven't taken your pills. Here.
Aren't you warm with all that?

Lucia:

Yes.
And lucid.
And most.

I think I'll be going.

{Lucia moves—fast to faster}

FALL

Lucia:

Can you see it? Can you see it? The light at the. The light that. The light. No. Again, but not before, yet before. It's like déjà vu. My body knows this dark. Knows what to do. Remember? No.

Mother:

When Lucia was a child she was just wild about halogen …

MHP:

As a primary light source?

Lucia:

Skin still warm. Hasn't been long. Yet. And I know. I know. I know something in the forecast calls for wanting. And forgetting. And night for months without dreams, sleep without stir, night without night without

Mother:

Regular old bulbs just wouldn't do for that child. And she kept the lamps on round the clock, even when she slept.

MHP:

Don't blame yourself. There was nothing you could have done.

Lucia:

Open my eyes and see nothing. Open my eyes and see nothing. Open my eyes and see nothing. Open my eyes and see nothing. Open. See. Nothing. Was something ever?

Mother:

Well, I don't believe that. She was so bright. So intense.

Lucia:

Circadian rhythm shifts. Sheep to squirrel. Drowse to sleep. Deep. [Yawn]

MHP:

Classic case. We'll go the usual route. In a few months she should be as good as …

Mother:

Lucia did everything with such dramatic flair. Do you know she wanted to be an actress? From the time she was three. Her name in lights.

Lucia:

Fallen.

Post-traumatic stress? Something repressed from childhood? Inability to cope with life pressures? Negative thinking? A self-destructive bent? Situational depression stemming from the devastating break-up of my unhappy relationship with the wrong X? Or could it just be PMS? What's the diagnosis this time?

As if
a binary situation.
The lamp is on.
It is off.
I am on. I am off.
Light. No light.
And I glide between currents paying the middle no mind.
Now I am only now.
Not then nor when.
No matter if my eyes are open.
Or closed.
Or looking.
Or not.
Most forgetting occurs in the first few moments.
And it has been long since.

[yawn]

{Lucia moves — brisk to trudge}

[gets into a bed or curls up, fetal position, on ground facing audience]

WINTER

[Lucia is lying still, eyes open, staring blankly outward]

Mother:

Daddy and I went to the Riverside for lunch yesterday. We saw your old friend. From high school ... oh what's her name ... she was in all the same activities as you ... ummm, Amy? Annie? Angie. That's it. Angie. Don't know what her last name is now that she's married. She's got a little one—almost three. They built in that big new development on the West Side. Cute little girl. Tow head. Looks just like him.

MHP:

Inadequate response to first line treatment.

Mother:

You always had so many nice young men calling on you.

MHP:

We'll increase to the maximum dose.

Mother:

Did I tell you Uncle Roger's retiring? He and Aunt Mimi are moving. To Arizona. The air there is better for her allergies. They just put their house up. They're looking at an adult community. Right on a golf course. Uncle Roger says he'll be able to just walk off his back deck and tee off. Daddy says they'd better get some of those special polycarbonate windows.

MHP:

If that doesn't work, we'll try an alternate first line.

Mother:

Oh snap out of it!

MHP:

And/or augment.

Mother:

Billy and Susan are coming for the weekend. Billy's going to help Daddy replace that back porch door and Susan and I are going over to the outlet stores to shop.

Lucia:

[sits up, snapping fingers, staring out, breaks and begins to speak]

Approximately fifteen human neurons have firepower equal to
    one D battery.
Beta waves — high frequency, low amp — are associated with
    arousal.
I am drawn to small portable electronic devices.
And flashlights.
It usually ends disastrously.
The therapists always said it was my self-destructive tendency.
The psychiatrist says my transmissions fail.
I just fire fire fire away.
But am not received.
Says I've been mistreated.
For years.
It's not uncommon, really.
To be not ground.
And undetected.

[snaps]

Angie was such a snobbish little bitch.

[snaps]

Tell Billy and Susan I say.

[snaps fingers again and lies back down]

{Stillness}

MHP:

The blood tests showed toxicity. I suppose you really weren't feeling well. We'll try something else.

SPRING

Lucia:

Once I was incandescent.

{Lucia moves—upright to forward}

LATE SPRING

MHP:

Do NOT miss a dose.

Mother:

Lucia's never been good at following directions. Her report cards. She always got check pluses in every other category. But "Cooperates and follows directions"? Check minus.

Lucia:

[sigh] Fluorescents.

Mother:

Spirited little thing she was. Always said she'd give us a run for our money. Had no idea.

MHP:

Do NOT stop taking your meds.

Mother:

Your hair's growing. Always liked the way it curls at the ends when it grows out. Frames that pretty face. You really ought to keep it a little longer, it's so boyish short.

MHP:

You'll need to be seen weekly.

Mother:

Evelyn told me a handsome young man moved in to Fraser's old place. She thinks he's single …

Lucia:

So you told him your lovely daughter will be outta psych soon and is just crazy to meet him?

[louder] Fluorescents.

Mother:

Well if you'd just try …

I'm telling everyone you're in Europe.

MHP:

Lucia's condition …

Mother:

We've had enough of your shenanigans.

MHP:

She needs time. She's ill.

Lucia:

I need light.
Flight.
Clip the wings
to save the girl.
Gray is better.
Dull is well.
Stuff a pill in me.
I am a
socket
now.
Grounded.
Empty.
Waiting
for a prong
that doesn't
come to
surge.

Mother:

Well it's not like she's got cancer. Or diabetes.

Lucia:

Beta beta beta beta beta beta
baby come back
what I wouldn't give for
a good
transistor

pen light

when I was a girl
fading
I used to poke holes in the bottom of
glow sticks
hold the string and
spin spin spin
til the dark was
interrupted
my
handspun aurora
burn me
to dawn
and if the liquid faded first
well

Mother:

I mean, she's always been moody. You don't have to call it a
disorder. Now she has an excuse.

MHP:

She's stable now. No moods.

[Lucia appears on video monitor]

Lucia (video):

Don't ever go to Europe! The food here in Europe is lousy! They make you take anti-psychotic drugs and if you refuse they'll never let you leave Europe! The other tourists here in Europe are fucking insane! At dinner today an elderly European woman tried to stab me with a spoon. She thought I was after her European pudding. They're just crazy about their diabetic butterscotch pudding here in Europe!

[quieter] This fucking European getaway was really overpriced.

Mother:

Well, good then.

Daddy was telling me that he saw an article in Sunday's paper about Feline Leukemia, it listed the symptoms and he's afraid Mitts might be sick. We're getting her tested next

Lucia (live performer):

Excuse me
but I seem to be
eclipsed.

{Lucia moves—fast to faster}

BODY/TALK/RADIO

Characters:

Eula Meltðown: live performer
ʃtreet venðor: an inflatable human form

Props:

table
handheld battery-operated toy radio with electronic beats and
flashing lights

Eula is twisting/contorting to loud music. Turns and notices audience.

[embarrassed] Ummm, hi. Have you been sitting there long? Really? That long? Oh god. I'm so embarrassed. Caught talking to myself ... again.

[to self] Ugghhh, Eula when are you going to learn? Do not objectify oneself in public. Reflect in solitude. As in ... alone.

You're doing it again.

[to audience] You won't tell anyone what I just said, right? I mean, I didn't realize I had an audience. I was just ... talking. [big exhale]

I just haven't been able to get the swing of "interior" monologue since I changed the way I talk.

[pause]

Oh, I haven't always talked like that. I used to, you know, use regular words and stuff. Like I am now. But it just wasn't working for me.

Nobody ever seemed to get me. I'm not sure why. Words all have neutral definitions, right? I say "cat," you know what a cat is. But somehow, when the words come from me, it's like I've made them up, or scrambled them. Or like when I speak I've somehow shifted the definitions in the dictionary one space down or something, so the meanings just don't line up the same. I say "cat," people think "a cause justifying war," not "a domesticated carnivorous mammal having retractile claws."

After I speak, people usually just stare at me blank and confused.

So I got this new way of talking.

[movement sequence]

[raised eyebrow, frowns]

Eula runs and picks up radio.

Aha.

[same movement sequence, but to radio beats]

[raised eyebrow again, nods for further emphasis, rushes into text]

Can you believe I had the guts to just say that to total strangers? Whew.

Eula moves closer to audience.

It's like now that I feel like I'm really communicating I can say anything that's on my mind. Because it's really mine. No one else has ever said that before in just that way. My talk doesn't have baggage. If I tell you [movement] you don't think about the way your friend, lover, boss, cousin says [movement] in an entirely different context. Or what [movement] would mean if you looked it up in the dictionary. I've solved my term/meaning alignment problem. I mean, I don't expect everyone to get me all the time. But the desire to be understood is really just an abstract piece of my concrete and total speech plan.

And if you just stare at me blank and confused, like you're doing right now, well, that's a valid response. You're telling me just as much as if you'd said, "Ew gross" or "Right on." Or took this as an opportunity to advocate the merits of cotton briefs ...

[movement sequence, radio beats]

Can you believe? Splitting up over a roach? But I really think it was symptomatic of our larger communication issues. I wasn't afraid of the roach. I had visceral revulsion to what the fact of the roach in my cupboard represented. Nasty flat-bodied pest. Filthy little legs traversing my dry goods. Who wouldn't jump away and scream? In an expressive sense, the large body movements indicating fear and disgust are actually quite similar. [mimes fear, disgust] I understand why my reaction might have looked like fear to one who didn't know, but to persist after I'd explained …

It'd be difficult to stay with someone who erroneously believed I was afraid of roaches, but I could probably overlook it if it had been an isolated incident.

I had no choice but to break it off. So to avoid confusion, I quite simply said:

[movement, radio beats]

[to self] Was I too harsh?

Now, I've been thinking a lot about nonverbal communication. For a long time. Since high school French class. Monsieur was an expert in "body language," though his knowledge of French was questionable.

Monsieur spent most of our class time calling us on "inappropriate" physical behavior—in English! Now, I have this pointy bone mass on the side of my left knee so I can only cross my legs comfortably left over right, and Monsieur was convinced this meant I wasn't paying attention, because, as anyone could plainly see, I was closing my body away from him—a sure sign of disinterest and rejection. Our class was plagued by offenses—slumping, arm crossing, gaze aversion … And Monsieur was bent on sending us out in the world well aware of the nuances of our physical behavior.

[pause]

Like, did you know that at a business lunch or interview it's fatal to salt your food before tasting it because this indicates haste? Uh huh.

And while scratching one's nose could just mean that one has an itchy nose, it could also mean one is telling a lie. So never scratch your nose when saying something you really mean.

And there are actual studies that show standard patterns in elevator proxemics. Yeah. There are these unwritten rules about where you're supposed to stand and how — two people lean against walls, four occupy the corners, any more, fill in the middle. And the proper stance for the elevator is the "fig leaf position": hands, purses, briefcases hang down in front of the body. Do not touch the person next to you, get as tall and skinny as possible, and look up at the floor indicator. No joke, I've tested it. People get really bugged out if you just walk on and don't turn around to face the door and just look at them …

You really gotta be aware of this stuff.

It all really started to freak me out. I left four years of high school French unable to speak a sentence and with a horrible sense that I was going through life saying things with my body without even knowing it. I became a bit obsessed. And almost cataleptic.

[rigid movement sequence]

Til the day I got my radio …

Lights up on inflatable figure at folding table with assorted objects on it. The table should be somewhere sidestage, visible but not in the main performance space so it can be revealed, then dimmed and taken out of the visual for the remainder of the performance.

Eula moves backward toward table quickly, and motions moving backward but looking as she would if walking forward—as if she's in rewind. Eula makes her way over to the table stiff-limbed, looking down. She puts the radio on the table and pretends it has been there all along and she has never seen it before. Peruses items on table, gaze settles on radio. Mumbles about wanting to see the radio—improvisation, e.g., "I think I'd like to purchase that radio." Volume increases. "Oh, you don't understand me." Straightens a bit. Gestures her way through the purchase of radio. Presses button, beats begin. Gestures thank you. Hugs inflatable figure. Bops back to center with radio. Lights fade on silhouette/table.

[fast forward back to main performance space]

My entire life changed after that. I took the radio everywhere with me. I realized it was my key to successful communication. My little red radio—and my body.

Really. There have only been three times including that day that I ever really successfully communicated exactly what I wanted to in my whole life. The first time was when I flipped off Sister Agnes in second grade because she told me I was not to speak a word for the rest of the afternoon because I'd inadvertently said something to another little girl that led her to believe she was born male. And I didn't think Sister Agnes was looking, but I guess she was and, man, did she get what I was saying, and man did I ever get it! Then she called my parents and told them I might be "disturbed" because I said terrible things and gleefully giggled while she whacked my wrist with her wooden ruler. But I was just so happy to be understood.

And there was that time I mooned …

Well, anyway … Once I found my radio it all made perfect sense. Words don't work. Body does. The beats are magic. Knowing all that, how else could I talk? It was such a rush. I started to talk all the time. And I had a lot to say.

[movement sequence, particularly acrobatic]

It's hard work talking like this. And I've never quite figured out the phone. And I don't have a job anymore. But it's not like I was so good at keeping jobs, anyway. The only one I really miss is the fast food joint. I mean, the job itself pretty much sucked. But I left every shift smelling like fries and pickles so I'd go ride the mall elevator for an hour or so, and I had so many successful olfactory communications—most of them positive, I think. Real success was when I induced cravings. When I thought that was happening, I'd get off and follow them to the food court to be sure. Those days were so good! So, at work, when people had trouble getting their burgers because I couldn't serve them til they ordered on my terms, my boss said maybe this wasn't a good career for me, given my unique expressive sensibility, and maybe I should try balloon-o-grams or something … I think I just needed more practice.

It's taken a while to really get the hang of this. But I think now it's working for me. I mean, I think at first the talk was really speaking me. But now, I'm doing the talking.

[radio beats and movement sequence]

Eula winks at audience, slumps when she realizes they don't get it.

Well, I'd rather be misunderstood on my own terms than constantly failing with somebody else's.

Eula moves to chair, assumes "The Thinker" pose.

Lights fade. Tick tock sound. Lights up.

[in astonishment] I'm just a link in a chain. How'd I not know? Oh man. I'm just a walking non-sequitur.

[to self] You can stop objectifying yourself now. You've got them. [points to audience] Okay stop it. Talk to them. Better yet, shut up and listen for a change. You could talk the teeth off a saw, Eula, and you've never had a real conversation. Attempts at communication fail because you talk too much.

[to audience] Umm, I guess it's your turn ...

Lights fade.

Production Notes

"And I'm Not Jenny" can be performed by one or more persons, with or without the digital images as a backdrop. The series has been performed in San Francisco, Seattle, Milwaukee, Atlanta, and Athens, GA, and via video stills and audio in Auckland, New Zealand.

"BeRemainBecome" was written and performed for Exponent: Women/Art/Power at the Clayton Street Gallery in Athens, GA in 2000.

"Vice Versa" was first performed at The Elvis Room in Portsmouth, NH in 1998. Subsequent places of performance include Boston, San Francisco, Plymouth, NH, and Athens, GA.

"BODY/TALK/RADIO" was written and performed for the Warehouse Collective's "Viewpoints" show at Canopy Studio in Athens, GA in 2002.

Acknowledgments

Thanks to the curators who hosted performances of material from this book. Many thanks to Paul Rogalus and Justin Chin for first helping me find my way off the page. Thanks to Ethan Paquin and Slope Editions for bringing performance to the page. Thanks to my advisors in the Goddard MFA-IA: Ruth Wallen, Beverly Naidus, Catherine Lord, Keith Hennessy, Daniel Alexander Jones and Pam Hall. Thanks to my dear friends and collaborators in the Warehouse Collective: Julie Rothschild, Laura Glenn and Lisa Yaconelli. Thanks to Kevin Strickland for collaboration, thrifting adventures and cue card holding with flair. Thanks to Jennifer Arave and Janice Perry for artistic support, friendship and humor. Thanks to Julie Page for everything for all these years. Thanks to Trish McDermott, the best role model a little girl could have asked for. Many many thanks to Walter and Maureen Rebele for all the love, support and encouragement. Very special thanks to Brian, collaborator in everything that matters, and to Brynne and Beckett for being everything that matters.